Natural Wonders of the World

YELLOWSTONE NATIONAL PARK

by Kelly Anne White

FOCUS READERS

FOCUS READERS

WWW.FOCUSREADERS.COM

Copyright © 2018 by Focus Readers, Lake Elmo, MN 55042. All rights reserved. No part of this book may be reproduced or utilized in any form or by any means without written permission from the publisher.

Focus Readers is distributed by North Star Editions:
sales@northstareditions.com | 888-417-0195

Produced for Focus Readers by Red Line Editorial.

Content Consultant: Jeffrey R. Walker, PhD, Professor of Earth Science, Vassar College

Photographs ©: YinYang/iStockphoto, cover, 1; ferrantraite/iStockphoto, 4–5; Red Line Editorial, 6; Carol M. Highsmith/Carol M. Highsmith's America Project/Carol M. Highsmith Archive/Library of Congress, 9; lucky-photographer/iStockphoto, 10–11; pawel.gaul/iStockphoto, 12–13; Agil_Leonardo/iStockphoto, 14; Bertl123/iStockphoto, 17; Bobbushphoto/iStockphoto, 18–19; 1Tomm/iStockphoto, 20; mlharing/iStockphoto, 23; robertcicchetti/iStockphoto, 24–25; BirdofPrey/iStockphoto, 26; michieldb/iStockphoto, 29

ISBN
978-1-63517-518-9 (hardcover)
978-1-63517-590-5 (paperback)
978-1-63517-734-3 (ebook pdf)
978-1-63517-662-9 (hosted ebook)

Library of Congress Control Number: 2017948106

Printed in the United States of America
Mankato, MN
November, 2017

ABOUT THE AUTHOR

Kelly Anne White is the author of *The Bible Adventure Book of Scavenger Hunts*. She is a former editor at Kirkus Media and a contributor for HarperCollins. For 15 years, Kelly was executive editor of *Girls' Life* magazine. She lives in Baltimore, and her new favorite oldies movie is *Yellowstone Kelly*.

TABLE OF CONTENTS

CHAPTER 1
A Magical Place 5

IT'S A WONDER!
Norris Geyser Basin 10

CHAPTER 2
Volcanic Beginnings 13

CHAPTER 3
Home on the Park 19

CHAPTER 4
A Park for All 25

Focus on Yellowstone National Park • 30
Glossary • 31
To Learn More • 32
Index • 32

CHAPTER 1

A MAGICAL PLACE

The **geysers** spray high into the sky. Muddy holes in the ground bubble and burp. Solid waterfalls spill like thick, white icing. Wildflowers bloom on hillside meadows. Meanwhile, bison herds roam in wide, golden fields. The scenery looks like it popped from the pages of a storybook. But this is Yellowstone National Park.

Yellowstone National Park is known for its many features, such as the Grand Prismatic Spring.

The park includes nearly 3,500 square miles (9,100 sq km) of land. It mostly covers the northwest corner of Wyoming.

MAP OF YELLOWSTONE PARK

Yellowstone is one of the biggest US national parks. Roads connect visitors to the main attractions.

However, Yellowstone also crosses into Montana and Idaho. Each state features some of the park's wonders.

The Grand Canyon of the Yellowstone is gaping and curvy. Water rushing through it forms the Upper Falls and Lower Falls. Nearly 300 other waterfalls grace the park's many trails. But waterfalls are not the only water features in the park.

Yellowstone has hundreds of active geysers. This is more than anywhere else in the world. The most popular geyser is called Old Faithful. It earned its name because it erupts regularly. Every hour or so, it shoots a fountain of hot, steamy water 180 feet (55 m) in the air.

Even hotter are the park's thousands of hot springs, which can sometimes reach the boiling point. The Grand Prismatic Spring is one of the most stunning. It boasts bands of brilliant colors. Bacteria living in the water create neon green, bright yellow, and shocking orange around an electric-blue center.

Mud pots are another of Yellowstone's features. Some are nicknamed "paint pots." That's because iron particles in the mud give them pink, gray, and beige tints. The muddy puddles sputter and spurt. Some stink like rotten eggs. The smell comes from the gases that gurgle in the mud.

The terraces at Mammoth Hot Springs look like a grand staircase.

Water sometimes falls over the terraces at Mammoth Hot Springs. The terraces are platforms made of limestone. They seem solid, but they are shape-shifters. They slowly change shape and color along with heat conditions. The same is true for many of Yellowstone's natural wonders.

IT'S A WONDER!

NORRIS GEYSER BASIN

With underground temperatures exceeding 400 degrees Fahrenheit (204°C), Norris Geyser Basin is Yellowstone's hottest area. Underground steam pressure vibrates the surface. Steam vents, called **fumaroles**, hiss from the mountainsides.

The basin has many geysers large and small. The tallest is Steamboat Geyser. It is taller than Old Faithful. Steamboat erupts to nearly 400 feet (122 m). That's taller than the Statue of Liberty.

Nearby are clear pools of blue water. But they might turn to sputtering pots of mud overnight. Some of the area's hot springs crackle. One cave even spews boiling green brew.

The thermal features at Norris Geyser Basin change every day.

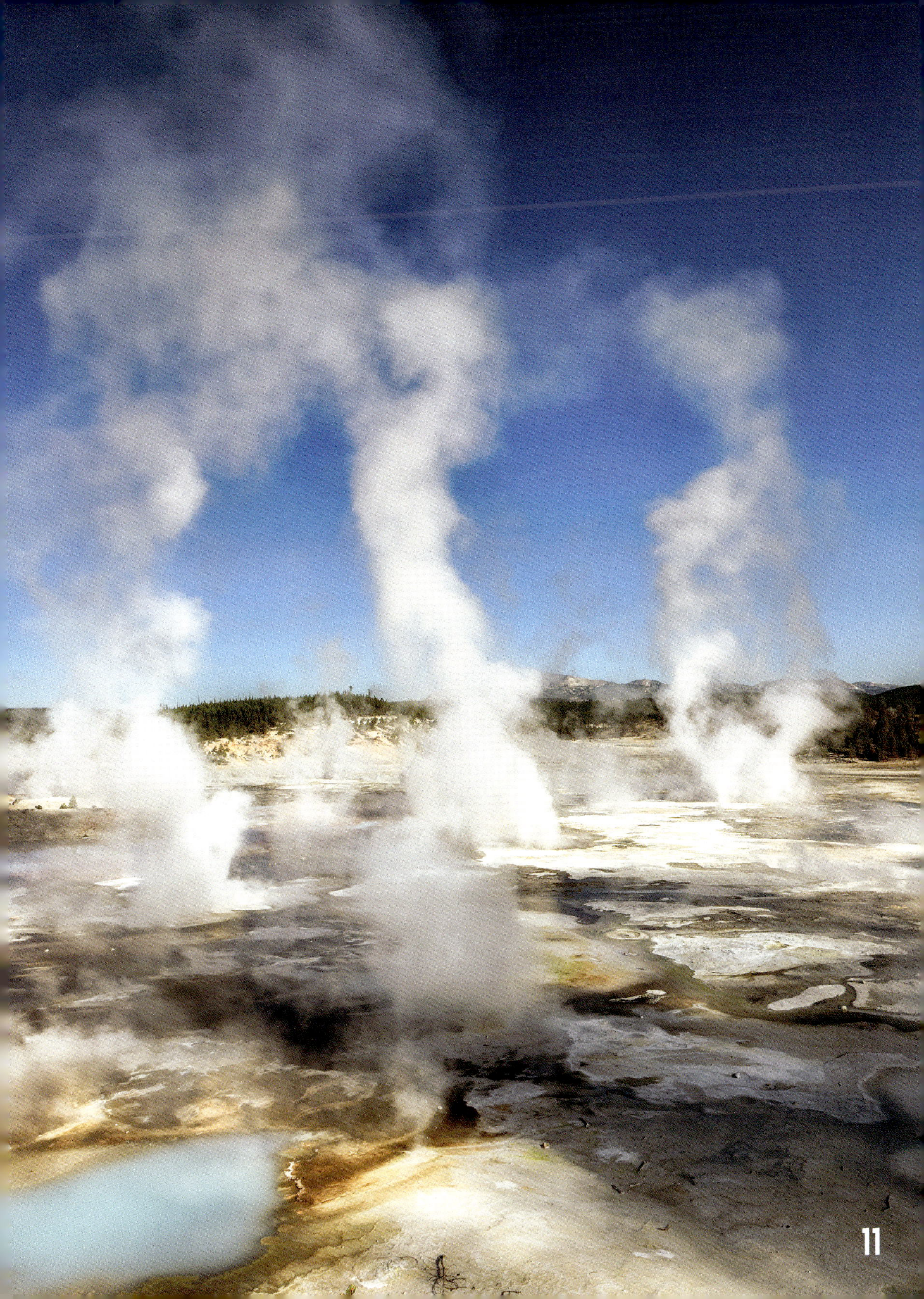

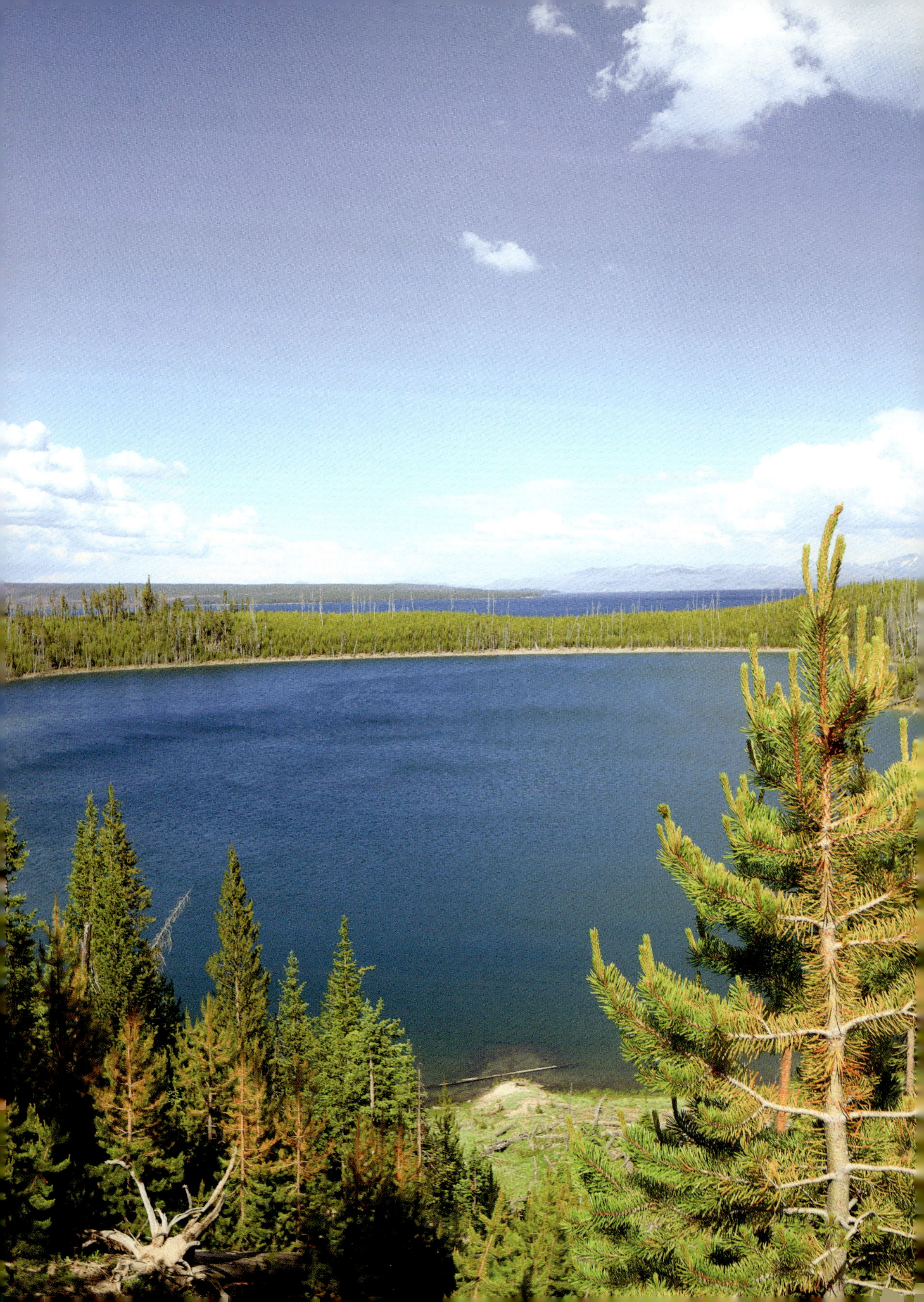

CHAPTER 2

VOLCANIC BEGINNINGS

A trio of huge volcanoes helped form the land at Yellowstone. The last one erupted more than 500,000 years ago. Each volcano spewed out **molten** rock. Then the earth's crust caved in beneath them. These volcanic craters are called calderas. Much of Yellowstone National Park rests inside the three giant calderas.

Scenic landscapes have developed within the calderas at Yellowstone.

Yellowstone Caldera is the largest volcano in North America. It's an active hot spot. **Magma** still boils below the surface. It heats the groundwater. That's

THE YELLOWSTONE CALDERA

what causes the park's geysers, hot springs, mud pots, and fumaroles.

Three major ice ages also occurred in the area. Thick ice took over the land. The last ice age ended approximately 13,000 years ago. As the **glaciers** melted, they sculpted mountains and plateaus. They widened canyons and valleys.

Earthquakes also shifted the land and its waterways. The Hebgen Lake earthquake of 1959 caused a massive landslide in Yellowstone. Earthquakes are still common in the park today. Thousands of earthquakes occur in Yellowstone each year. However, most are too small for visitors to feel.

Fires affect the park's ever-changing landscape as well. Park workers once saw forest fires as a threat. But they learned natural fires are important to renewing plant growth. Now they let the fires burn.

To protect Yellowstone, US lawmakers made it the first national park. President

LIBERTY CAP

In the 1800s, explorers found a cone-shaped tower. They thought it looked like a giant hat from the Revolutionary War (1775–1783). So they called it Liberty Cap. The tower is near Mammoth Terraces. It is made of limestone, just like the terraces. Hot water forced the limestone up from the ground. Over a long time, the cone grew bigger and bigger. One day, it stopped. But it surely left its mark.

The Lower Falls of the Grand Canyon of the Yellowstone is 308 feet (94 m) tall.

Ulysses S. Grant signed the Yellowstone National Park Protection Act in 1872. The act ensured the area would continue in its natural state. Developers would not be allowed to claim the land. Hunting, mining, and lumbering were also banned.

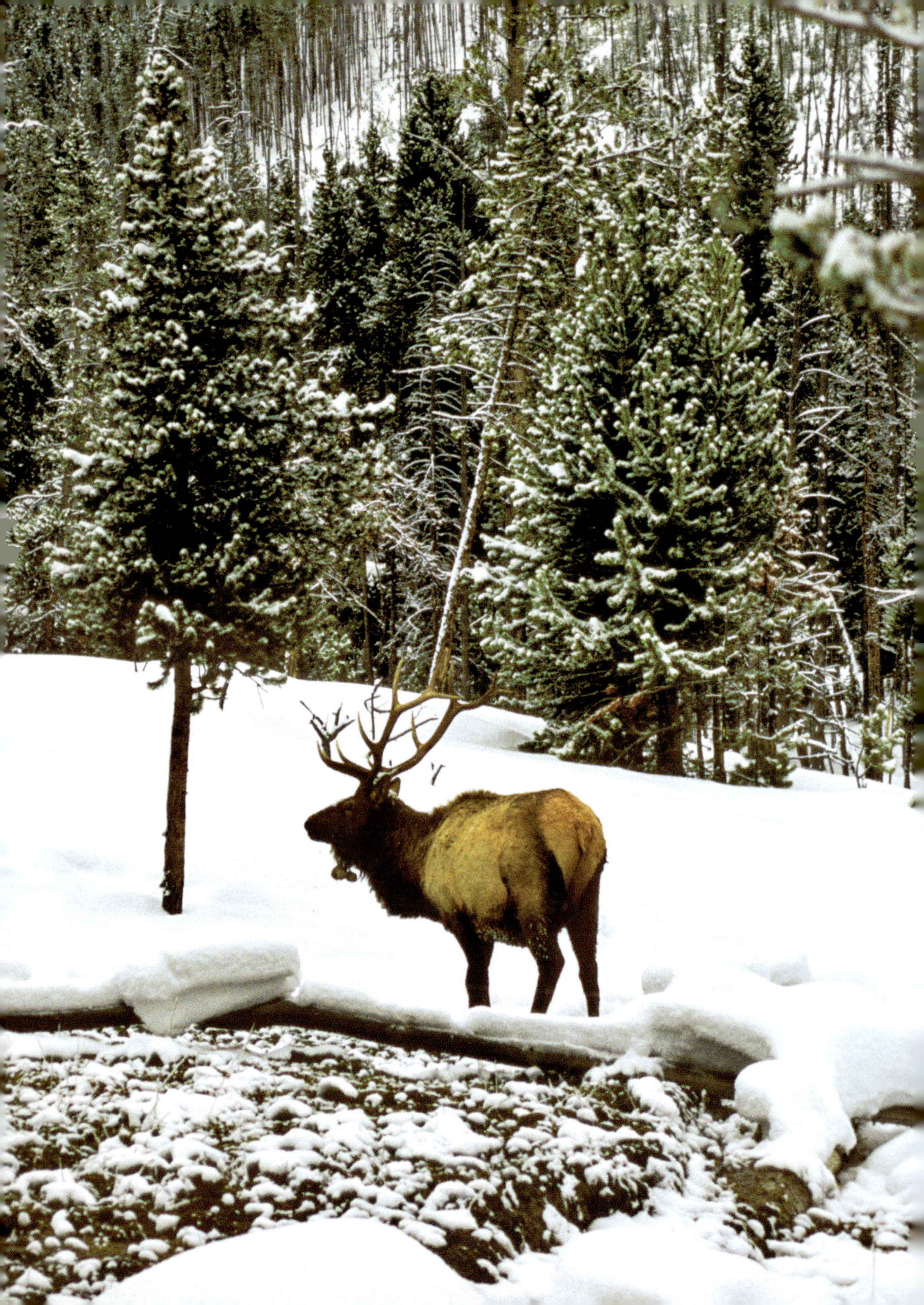

CHAPTER 3

HOME ON THE PARK

Parts of Yellowstone National Park's terrain are volcanic rock. But much of the land is covered by rich soil. That soil supports plant life. This vegetation promotes a bustling animal population. It's not unusual to spot wildlife in Yellowstone, especially in its valleys.

An elk roams Yellowstone National Park in the winter.

A bison grazes in a prairie at Yellowstone.

In all, more than 60 types of mammals live in Yellowstone. The park is home to most of the elk in the United States. Bison herds have lived in the area since prehistoric times. Other common mammals include antelope, deer, and moose. You might also find beavers, bighorn sheep, mountain lions, or wolves.

Some of the park's animals eat meat. Plant eaters have many options for food, too. They might dine in aspen groves, rows of cottonwood trees, or grassy fields. Bark, berries, and fir are plentiful. Pinecones, sagebrush, spruce twigs, and wild strawberries are also on the menu.

Beds of wildflowers decorate meadows, hills, and valleys. Flowers bloom mostly in summer. The blossoms are as varied and vibrant as their names. Some are called elephant's-head, fairy slipper, and monkey flower. The wildflowers' sweet scents attract critters. Hummingbirds, butterflies, and bumblebees are drawn to their nectar. So are grizzly bears.

Yellowstone makes for an ideal home for many birds. Bald eagles, ospreys, and falcons keep nests in the park. Ravens and hawks soar over the land. Smaller birds flutter close to trees and meadows. Magpies, chickadees, gray jays, and bluebirds make a chorus. Woodpeckers

THE NIGHT SKY

The night sky above Yellowstone is a theater for stargazers. There is no "light pollution." Light from buildings and streetlamps can brighten the night skies over many towns. But at Yellowstone, the night sky is unpolluted. Gazers get clear views of the Milky Way. They can watch Jupiter, Saturn, and Venus rise and set. And they can see all of these things without a telescope.

The great gray owl lives in the forests at Yellowstone.

add **percussion**. Birds also spend time near the park's rivers and lakes. **Waterfowl** include geese, loons, ducks, swans, and pelicans. Approximately 300 bird species have been spotted at Yellowstone.

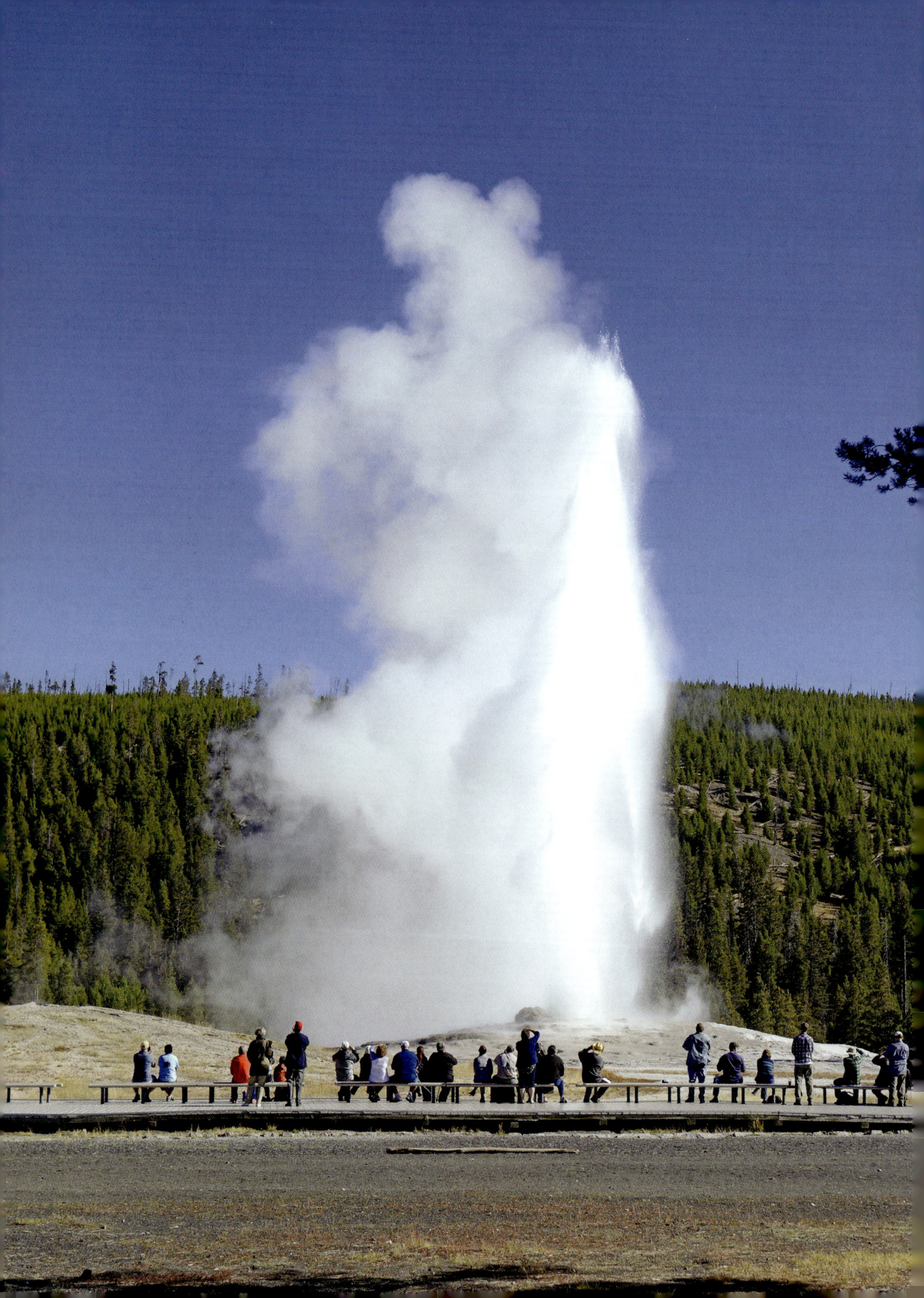

CHAPTER 4

A PARK FOR ALL

People love to explore Yellowstone's beauty. Campers and hikers flock to the park. It is a great spot for outdoor activities. Biking, boating, and horseback riding are especially popular. In winter, some visitors tour the park on snowshoes or cross-country skis.

Visitors admire Old Faithful at Yellowstone National Park.

Boardwalks help tourists admire Yellowstone's natural wonders up close.

During fishing season, many people catch trout in the park's lakes, rivers, and streams. Yellowstone Lake is a favorite fishing spot. Swimming in the lake is not allowed. However, the park has two safe swimming holes.

Most of the park is in its natural state. But there are also roads, hotels, and other facilities. These are for the park's millions of annual visitors. Visitors are expected to respect Yellowstone's natural state.

Likewise, Yellowstone's caretakers have learned to let nature take its course. For example, they once tried to control the wolf population. This took place through the early 1900s. Park workers feared the wolves would feed on too many elk. But they now know predatory wolves are important to the **ecosystem**. Wolves were brought back to the park in 1995.

Yellowstone remains under a watchful eye. The Endangered Species Act protects the grizzlies and other animals. Officials keep an eye on bison and elk for health issues. They check water quality.

They also protect rare plants and monitor climate change. Ongoing research of all sorts is carried out.

The National Park Service oversees the care of Yellowstone National Park. Other agencies also care for the park. Yellowstone Forever is a nonprofit agency

UNPREDICTABLE YELLOWSTONE

Most people agree that Yellowstone National Park is lovely. But some also say the area is **volatile**. Yellowstone is, after all, a volcano. This is why scientists track the park's **seismic** activity. By tracking changes, experts can predict possible eruptions. Even so, experts say an eruption won't happen for at least a thousand years.

Yellowstone has scenery that is unlike anywhere else in the world.

that partners with the National Park Service. Yellowstone Forever has dozens of programs to benefit the park. Projects include high-altitude archaeology and fish conservation. Indeed, Yellowstone National Park is well loved.

FOCUS ON YELLOWSTONE NATIONAL PARK

Write your answers on a separate piece of paper.

1. Pretend you are a reporter writing about Yellowstone. Write a headline about one of the park's wonders.

2. If you visited Yellowstone National Park, which animals would you most hope to spot? Why?

3. Which natural events left huge craters called calderas in Yellowstone?
   - **A.** earthquakes
   - **B.** ice ages
   - **C.** volcanic eruptions

4. What is the relationship between wolves and elk in Yellowstone?
   - **A.** The animals are an important part of nature's predator-prey chain.
   - **B.** The two species never cross paths in the park.
   - **C.** Wolves provide protection to the elk that are threatened.

Answer key on page 32.

GLOSSARY

ecosystem
The collection of living things in a natural area.

fumaroles
Vents in the earth's surface, usually near volcanic regions, from which steam and gases are released.

geysers
Holes in the ground that spew hot water and steam.

glaciers
Large, slow-moving bodies of ice.

magma
Hot, melted rock under Earth's surface.

molten
Melted by intense heat.

percussion
A striking or tapping sound.

seismic
Relating to Earth's vibrations.

volatile
Likely to erupt violently.

waterfowl
Birds that live on or near water such as ducks or geese.

TO LEARN MORE

BOOKS

Carson, Mary Kay. *Park Scientists: Gila Monsters, Geysers, and Grizzly Bears in America's Own Backyard*. Boston: Houghton Mifflin Harcourt, 2014.

Mattern, Joanne. *Yellowstone: America's First National Park*. Egremont, MA: Red Chair Press, 2018.

Peabody, Erin. *A Weird and Wild Beauty: The Story of Yellowstone, the World's First National Park*. New York: SkyPony Press, 2016.

NOTE TO EDUCATORS

Visit www.focusreaders.com to find lesson plans, activities, links, and other resources related to this title.

INDEX

birds, 21–23
bison, 5, 20, 27

calderas, 13–14
climate change, 28
conservation, 27–29

earthquakes, 15
elk, 20, 27

fires, 16
flowers, 5, 21
fumaroles, 10, 15

geysers, 5, 7, 10, 15
Grand Canyon of the Yellowstone, 7
Grand Prismatic Spring, 8

hot springs, 8, 10, 15

Liberty Cap, 16

Mammoth Hot Springs, 9, 16
mud pots, 5, 8, 10, 15

Norris Geyser Basin, 10

Old Faithful, 7, 10

plants, 19, 21, 28

volcanoes, 13, 19, 28

waterfalls, 5, 7
wolves, 20, 27
Wyoming, 6

Answer Key: 1. Answers will vary; 2. Answers will vary; 3. C; 4. A